# Echo Mentis

## The Mind's Echo

"Echo Mentis, 'The Mind's Echo,' will guide you through the profound connection between soul, spirit, and consciousness, on a journey of deep self-exploration and introspection into the profound realm of our mind. This book unveils ancient secrets for personal growth, opening the doors to a metaphysical journey toward self-realization."

## Dedication

*To those who dare to tread the path of self-exploration and inner growth, to those seeking the connection between soul, spirit, and consciousness, this book is dedicated. May you find inspiration and wisdom within these pages as you embark on your mystical journey toward self-realization.*

# CONTENTS

Introduction       p. 9

- The importance of personal introspection and self-knowledge.
- Explanation of the concept of echo mentis and the idea of an inner echo.

Chapter 1: Shades of the Mind.       p. 16

- Exploring the complexity and diversity of mental processes.
- The interaction between thoughts, emotions, and intuitions.
- The duality of mind-consciousness.

Chapter 2: Mental Entropy.       p. 32

- The nature of changes and fluctuations in the mind.
- The importance of addressing mental entropy for well-being and growth.

Chapter 3: Vibrational Resonance.       p. 40

- Delving into the concept of vibrational resonance in the spirit.
- How our vibrations influence our mental and emotional state.

Chapter 4: Architectures of the Mind.       p. 51

- Exploring the various layers of the mind and the subconscious.
- The importance of understanding mental structures to transform limiting thought patterns.
- Intuition.

Chapter 5: Exploring the Soul.       p. 72

- Accessing the depths of the human soul.
- Integrating the different aspects of the soul: light and shadow.

## Chapter 6: Practices of Awareness.                                    p.  90

- Tools and techniques for cultivating awareness and self-observation.
- Meditation, mindfulness, and other practices to connect with The Mind's Echo.

## Chapter 7: Transformation and Realization                    p. 101

- The potential for personal growth and development through introspection.
- How to integrate inner experience into everyday life.

## Conclusion:                                                          p. 111

- Encouragement to continue the journey of discovering the mind and spirit.

# INTRODUCTION (PART ONE)

## THE IMPORTANCE OF PERSONAL INTROSPECTION AND SELF-KNOWLEDGE

The human mind is an unknown galaxy, an intricate labyrinth of thoughts, emotions, and perceptions that stretches to infinity. Every day, we venture into this inner universe, often without realizing the extraordinary depths it holds. But what if we took some time to explore these uncharted regions? What could we discover as we delve into the abyss of our thoughts? This is the journey we will embark on together in 'Echo Mentis: The Mind's Echo.'

In an era where we are constantly immersed in a whirlwind of information and distractions, it's easy to get lost in the noise of the external world. Our fast-paced lives often lead us to act impulsively, make hasty decisions, and pursue goals that may not truly reflect who we are. In this daily frenzy, the art of personal introspection and self-knowledge is often neglected, yet it is essential for achieving a more fulfilling and authentic life.

Why should we delve into the depths of our mind? The answer is as simple as it is profound: because this is where the key to a meaningful life resides. Personal introspection is not just an intellectual exercise but a gateway to greater self-awareness. It is a journey of self-exploration that allows us to shed light on those dark corners of our psyche, embrace our contradictions, and discover the beauty of our uniqueness.

The human mind is an infinitely changing canvas, a landscape in constant evolution. It is the place where dreams are born and fears are generated, where the threads of hope and despair intertwine. But too often, the mind is uncharted territory, a continent we only superficially map. In 'Echo Mentis,' we will delve into the depths of this unknown land, unveiling the intricate meanderings of mental processes.

We will begin our journey with a simple yet profound question: who are we truly? This seemingly elementary question is the starting point for an odyssey in search of self-knowledge. For, as the Greek philosopher Socrates asserted, 'Know thyself' is the supreme commandment, the starting point for all forms of personal growth.

Throughout the pages of this book, we will explore the complexity of the human mind, highlighting the nuances that make it so fascinating and mysterious. Through the lens of introspection, we will take a look at the interactions between our thoughts, the emotions that overwhelm us, and the intuitions that guide us.

We will discover how the mind is an ever-expanding universe, and how our understanding of ourselves is destined to grow and develop over time. Yet, to embark on this journey, we must also confront the duality that exists between the mind and consciousness.

But this is only the beginning of our journey. In the following pages, we will explore mental entropy, the nature of changes and fluctuations in the mind, and the importance of addressing it for our well-being and growth.

Continuing, we will uncover the fascinating concept of vibrational resonance in the spirit, and how our vibrations influence our mental and emotional state. Through this exploration, we will begin to understand that we can modulate our vibrations to create a more fulfilling reality.

In the next chapter, we will immerse ourselves in the architectures of the mind, unveiling the various layers of the mind and the subconscious. Understanding these mental structures is crucial for transforming limiting thought patterns that trap us in self-destructive cycles.

And then, our journey will take us to explore the depths of the human soul, to access its darker and brighter dimensions. We will discover how integrating these different facets of the soul is essential for our personal growth.

Subsequently, we will examine practices of awareness, providing tools and techniques to cultivate mindfulness and self-observation. Meditation, mindfulness, and other practices will help us connect with The Mind's Echo, explore its mysteries, and understand its potential.

Finally, we will reach the final stage of our journey, where we will explore the potential for personal growth and development through introspection. We will learn how to integrate inner experience into everyday life, turning our self-knowledge into action and realization.

This is the path we will embark on together in "The Mind's Echo: Exploring the Unknown." Be prepared to delve into the depths of your mind and discover the unlimited potential within you. The road may be winding at times, but the reward will be a life lived with awareness, authenticity, and profound satisfaction. Are you ready? Then, let's begin our journey into the unknown.

# INTRODUCTION (PART TWO)

## EXPLANATION OF THE CONCEPT OF 'ECHO MENTIS' AND THE NOTION OF AN INNER ECHO

Every mind is a unique landscape, a universe of thoughts, feelings, and experiences. Yet, within the blurred contours of this mental vastness lies an intriguing concept: the echo of the mind, 'echo mentis.' It's an idea that invites us to consider our minds not as a static collection of thoughts but as a place where the vibrations of our thoughts and emotions resonate like in a grand auditorium of the soul.

Imagine the mind as a tranquil lake. Every thought, every emotion, is a small stone we throw into this lake. Each stone creates ripples, and these ripples propagate across the water's surface, interacting, overlapping, creating an intricate tapestry of movements. The echo mentis is like the reflection of these ripples, a reflection that can reveal much about our inner world.

To fully grasp the echo mentis, we must embrace the idea that our mind is not static but in constant motion. Every thought, every emotion, every experience that passes through our mind generates a vibration, an energy that weaves into the very fabric of our being. These vibrations are not fleeting but leave an imprint, an echo that continues to resonate even when the original thought has faded.

The echo mentis is like a memory of the soul, a record of our experiences and moods. It is the reverberation of our joys and sorrows, our hopes and fears. When we become aware of this inner echo, we enter a territory deep and rich in meaning.

Imagine yourself in a quiet room surrounded by glass walls. Every time you speak a word or express a thought, the sound spreads through the glass and is permanently recorded. Over time, the room fills with echoes of your past words and thoughts. These echoes can influence your perception of the present and your future choices.

In our minds, something similar happens. Every thought, every emotion, every decision leaves an echo. These echoes can affect our self-esteem, our behaviors, and even our overall well-being. The first step to understanding and harnessing the echo of the mind to our advantage is to become aware of its existence.

In addition to awareness, the echo of the mind also offers us the opportunity to explore the past and present of our minds more deeply. We can dig into the layers of these mental recordings and uncover the roots of our behaviors and reactions. This is a process of self-analysis that requires patience and dedication, but the rewards are profound.

Think of an echo in the mountains. When you speak, the echo responds, but it does so with a slight delay. It's as if the mountain takes your message, reflects it, and then returns it. So, it is with the echo of the mind. The answers to our deepest questions may take time to manifest, but if we listen carefully, we can feel the awakening of the answers within us.

But the echo of the mind is more than just a recording of past experiences. It is also a reflection of our aspirations and future desires. When we envision our ideal future, when we dream and plan, we are casting stones into the lake of the mind. And these stones generate ripples that, over time, create an image of our desired destiny.

The notion of an inner echo reminds us that we are creators of our reality. We can shape our future through the thoughts and emotions we cultivate today. But to do so, we must tune in to the echo of the mind, listen carefully to it, and work in collaboration with it.

In the book, we will explore how we can use this idea of the echo of the mind to enhance our lives. We will discover how to become architects of our minds, creating thoughts and emotions that lead us toward a more fulfilling reality.

# CHAPTER 1: SHADES OF THE MIND

## EXPLORING THE COMPLEXITY AND DIVERSITY OF MENTAL PROCESSES.

The human mind is an uncharted territory, a vast and mysterious landscape of thoughts, emotions, and perceptions. It's a place where reality intertwines with imagination, where past and future dance in an eternal present. But how much do we truly know about it? Exploring the complexity and diversity of mental processes is like venturing into an intricate secret garden, a journey that will lead us to discover a world of nuances and intricate mechanisms.

*Thoughts as Strokes of Color*

Let's imagine the mind as an abstract painting, a blank canvas on which thoughts paint their strokes of color. Each thought is a different shade, a unique hue contributing to the overall picture of our mind. Some thoughts are bright and vibrant like the yellow of the sunrise, while others are dark and murky like a stormy gray sky.

These strokes of thought are never static. They blend, overlap, create new tones and shades. The mind is in constant motion, like a painting in continuous evolution. When we make an effort to explore the complexity of these thoughts, we discover they are like crystal spheres, each containing an entire universe of meaning.

## Emotions as Hidden Melodies

Alongside thoughts, emotions make up another fundamental part of our mental landscape. Imagine emotions as hidden melodies, notes resonating deep within the mind. Some melodies are joyful and cheerful, while others are melancholic or anxious. These melodies create the soundtrack of our inner life.

Emotions, like melodies, can be complex and nuanced. Joy may be mixed with a hint of sadness, love intertwined with fear. Often, we are only aware of the most prominent emotions, but by delving deeper into the mind, we can discover subtler melodies, the nuances of emotions interweaving in surprising ways.

## Perceptions as Tactile Strokes

In addition to thoughts and emotions, perceptions are another key element of our mind. Perceptions are like tactile strokes that connect us to the external world. Feeling the warmth of the sun on our skin, tasting the flavor of food, seeing the vibrant colors of a landscape - these are all sensory experiences enriching our mind. But perceptions are not limited to just the five senses. Perceptions also include our ability to sense the inner world, to reflect on our thoughts and emotions. This is where the mind becomes a tool of self-observation, allowing us to explore the depths of our being.

## The Dance of Connections

What truly makes the complexity of mental processes fascinating is the dance of connections that occur among thoughts, emotions, and perceptions. The synapses in our brain are like roads connecting different neighborhoods of a city. Thoughts travel along these roads, creating new pathways and connections.

These connections are what make us uniquely human. Our life experiences, our interactions with the world and others, shape the topography of our mind. Each connection is a piece of the puzzle, a tile fitting into the mosaic of our identity.

Exploring the complexity of mental processes also means understanding the external and internal influences shaping our minds. The environment in which you grow, the people you meet, the experiences you live - all contribute to forming your inner world.

*The Unique Mosaic of Each Individual*

It's important to emphasize that the mental mosaic of each individual is unique. No one has the same painting, the same melodies, or the same tactile strokes. The diversity of mental processes is what makes the world so rich and interesting. It's also what enables us to learn from others, share experiences, and grow as individuals.

Exploring the nuances of the mind is a captivating journey. It's like opening a series of nested Russian dolls, each containing a different secret. As we delve deeper into our inner world, we come closer to understanding who we truly are.

But this journey is never truly complete. The mind is an ever-evolving terrain, and the complexity of mental processes is an enigma that will never cease to surprise us. In the next chapter, we will explore the duality of mind and consciousness, another fascinating aspect of our mind. But for now, let's reflect on the beauty of the mind's nuances and how they make us unique in the vast landscape of human existence.

*The Mind as an Uncharted City*

Imagine the mind as an extensive, uncharted city with neighborhoods and hidden alleyways, each representing a different dimension of mental processes. Each street is a thought, each building an emotion, and each secret place represents a memory. Navigating this mental city requires a deep self-knowledge and a healthy dose of curiosity.

Within this mental city, thoughts are like people moving along the streets. Some are fleeting passersby, racing quickly and disappearing, while others take residence in the remote neighborhoods and become an integral part of the city itself. These thoughts don't exist in isolation; they intertwine, collide, and sometimes merge, creating new ideas and perspectives.

*Emotions as Vivid Colors*

In addition to thoughts, emotions paint the mental landscape with vibrant hues. Imagine emotions as vivid colors: the fiery red of anger, the serene blue of happiness, the murky gray of sadness. However, these emotions are never monolithic; they are nuanced and complex, blending together to create unique shades.

At the heart of this mental city, emotions are like artists painting the canvas of our experience. Joy can transform a gray day into a rainbow of positive emotions, while fear can cast a sinister shadow over every prospect. Exploring emotions leads us to discover the richness and depth of our inner world.

## Perceptions as Windows to the External World

Perceptions are the windows through which we observe the external world. Picture them as windows of a house, each offering a different perspective. Sight allows us to explore distant landscapes, touch connects us with the physical world, hearing captures life's melodies, taste introduces us to new flavors, and smell detects the surrounding fragrances.

But perceptions are not limited to the five senses. We can perceive the gentle caress of a happy memory or the sharp edge of past remorse. This internal perception capability allows us to explore the inner world with the same intensity as we explore the external world.

## Connections as Interweaving Roads

At the heart of this mental city, there are roads that intersect and branch out like branches of a tree. These roads represent connections between thoughts, emotions, and perceptions. Each connection is a bridge that links two parts of the mind, creating a path for thought and experience.

Connections are what make the human mind extraordinarily flexible and adaptable. We can create new pathways, break down old bridges, and construct new ones. Our ability to shape connections between thoughts is what enables us to learn, grow, and adapt to life's challenges.

## The Diversity of Human Minds

In our journey through the complexity and diversity of mental processes, it is important to emphasize that every mind is unique. Each individual has a unique mental map, with pathways, connections, and neighborhoods that belong to them alone. This diversity is what makes the world so rich and interesting.

However, despite the differences, there are also fundamental similarities that unite us as human beings. The ability to think, to experience emotions, and to perceive the world is universal. These mental processes are the common ground on which we build our human experiences.

## Explorers of the Inner World

The exploration of the complexity and diversity of mental processes is a lifelong journey. It's a fascinating adventure in which we are both the architect and the traveler. The mind is a continually evolving terrain, and each day it offers us new discoveries and surprises.

However, this journey is also a challenge. It requires self-observation, introspection, and a deep sense of curiosity. It means embracing the diversity of mental processes, recognizing that there is no single right path, and that complexity is an asset, not an obstacle.

In the upcoming pages, we will explore the interaction between thoughts, emotions, and intuitions, a captivating aspect of mental processes that will prompt us to reflect on the relationship between our mind and our consciousness. But for now, let us contemplate the wonder of the nuances of the mind and the infinite diversity that makes us uniquely human.

# THE INTERACTION BETWEEN THOUGHTS, EMOTIONS, AND INTUITIONS.

At the heart of our inner world, there is a perpetual dance, a symphony of thoughts, emotions, and intuitions that interweave and mutually influence each other. This complex interaction among the components of the human mind is one of the most fascinating and mysterious aspects of our existence.

## Thoughts as Bricks of the Mental Structure

Thoughts are like bricks with which we construct our mental edifice. Each thought is a stone that overlaps the previous one, building walls, floors, and ceilings within our mind. Thoughts are the words of a silent language that speak to our brain.

But what happens when these thoughts meet? When seemingly disparate ideas collide on the streets of our mind, new connections and synapses are born, shining like intersections in traffic. These encounters can trigger an explosion of creativity or a tide of confusion, depending on how we decide to manage them.

## Emotions as the Fuel for Thoughts

Emotions, on the other hand, act as the fuel for thoughts. They are the energy that powers the engine of the mind. When we are happy, our thoughts tend to be light and positive, like dancing soap bubbles in the air. When we are sad or angry, our thoughts can become dark clouds that obscure our perception of the world.

Emotions not only influence thoughts but can also significantly color them. A neutral thought can take on a positive or negative hue depending on the accompanying emotion. This interaction between emotions and thoughts can shape our worldview and our decisions.

*Intuitions as Silent Illuminations*

Intuitions, on the other hand, emerge silently and often unexpectedly. They are like a sudden light that pierces the darkness of our mind. Intuitions can come from a sudden connection between seemingly unrelated thoughts or from a deep emotion that translates into a sudden understanding.

One fascinating feature of intuitions is that they often seem to emerge out of nowhere, as if our mind were working beneath the surface to connect the dots and reveal a new perspective. These moments of insight can change the course of our thoughts and actions, leading us in new directions.

*The Synergy Among Mental Components*

But what truly makes the interaction between thoughts, emotions, and intuitions fascinating is their synergy. When these elements work together harmoniously, they can create a flow of awareness and understanding that goes beyond the sum of their parts.

Imagine solving a complex problem. Thoughts can process information and generate possible solutions, but it's often the emotion that determines which solution feels right to us. An intuition can then emerge like a flash, guiding us toward the best choice.

In other situations, emotions can amplify the power of a thought. When we are passionate or motivated, our thoughts can become powerful tools to achieve our goals. Emotions can give us the energy and determination necessary to pursue what we desire.

*Balancing the Interactions*

However, the interaction between thoughts, emotions, and intuitions is not always harmonious. Sometimes, thoughts can be overshadowed by negative emotions, or intuitions may seem to conflict with rational logic. In these situations, it's important to learn to balance these interactions.

Mindfulness and awareness can help us maintain a balance among these elements. When we become aware of our thoughts, emotions, and intuitions, we can observe them objectively, without being overwhelmed by emotions or blinded by thought habits. This allows us to explore the interactions at play and decide how to respond consciously.

A useful exercise for balancing these interactions is meditation. During meditation, we focus on our breath and observe the thoughts and emotions that arise without judgment. This helps us develop greater awareness of how thoughts and emotions interact with each other and how we can influence them through our mindful presence.

Furthermore, we can nurture our intuition through reflection and practice. Taking the time to reflect on past situations and consider how intuitions have contributed to decisions can help us develop greater confidence in our inner perceptions.

## The Art of Navigating the Mental Waves

Navigating the complex waves of thoughts, emotions, and intuitions is an art that requires practice and awareness. As navigators of our minds, we must be mindful of emotional currents and shifts in our thoughts.

When we can recognize how these interactions influence our experience, we become more adept at making conscious choices. We can choose to follow a positive thought, embrace a challenging emotion, or trust a deep intuition.

The key to effective navigation among these elements is mindfulness. When we are mindful of our thoughts, emotions, and intuitions, we have the power to shape our experience and make decisions that reflect our true essence.

## Shades of Human Experience

In the end, the interplay of thoughts, emotions, and intuitions is what adds shade to the human experience. It's like an orchestra playing a complex symphony, with each instrument contributing to the beauty of the music as a whole. Each element is crucial to our human experience, and learning to manage them harmoniously is an essential part of our journey of personal growth.

In the next chapter, we will delve into the intrinsic complexity of the human mind, exploring the constant interplay between cognitive processes and reflection upon them. We will analyze the dynamic dialogue between our ever-evolving thoughts and the awareness that guides them.

# THE DUALITY OF MIND-CONSCIOUSNESS

In the vast realm of the human being, there exists a mystery that has been with us since the dawn of consciousness: the duality of mind and consciousness. This duality is at the heart of our existence, an eternal dance between thought and the observation of that thought, between the uninterrupted flow of our thoughts and the consciousness that watches over them.

*The Mind as an Ivory Tower*

Imagine the mind as a majestic ivory tower that rises on the horizon of our consciousness. Inside this tower, there is a perpetual tumult of thoughts, images, and emotions. It's like a city that's always bustling, with streets crowded with thoughts moving swiftly, each with its own agenda and voice.

The mind is where the plots of our thoughts develop, where memories dance with expectations, and emotions choose their stages. It's where we envision the future and reflect on the past, where our dreams and fears take shape.

*Consciousness as the Light in the Tower*

At the same time, consciousness is the light that illuminates this ivory tower. It's the silent voice that observes and reflects on the thoughts that unfold in the mind. Consciousness is the silent witness to every thought, emotion, and perception that passes through the mind.

Imagine consciousness as a torch in the night. It casts a warm and gentle light on everything it encounters, making the inner world visible. It's this light of consciousness that allows us to become aware of our thoughts and emotions, to observe them without being completely engulfed by them.

*The Eternal Dance Between Mind and Consciousness*

The duality of mind and consciousness is like an eternal dance between two partners. The mind creates, stirs, strives, and immerses itself in thoughts, while consciousness observes, reflects, and remains silent. This dance is what makes us uniquely human. Other creatures may have a mind, but only humans have this ability of self-observation.

Often, in the hustle and bustle of daily life, we are completely immersed in the mind. We get swept away by thoughts, emotions, and concerns, losing sight of the light of consciousness. However, consciousness is always there, waiting to be rediscovered.

*Freedom in Awareness*

The duality of mind and consciousness grants us extraordinary power: the freedom of choice. When we become aware of the mind, we are no longer slaves to our thoughts and emotions. We can choose how to respond to thoughts, whether to give them credence or simply observe them without judgment.

Imagine being immersed in a storm of turbulent thoughts. The mind is like a turbulent ocean, with giant waves of worries and doubts. But consciousness is like a beacon in the storm, a guiding light that allows us to navigate through the waves without being overwhelmed by them.

When we become aware of the duality of mind and consciousness, we can learn to govern the mind rather than be governed by it. We can choose the thoughts we nurture and those we let go. This is a form of inner freedom that allows us to live more authentically and consciously.

## The Art of Meditation and Mindfulness

One of the paths to explore this duality is through the practice of meditation and mindfulness. During meditation, we focus on our breath and observe the thoughts that arise without judgment. This practice allows us to cultivate awareness of the mind in action.

Awareness is like an inner compass that guides us within the mind. It helps us identify thoughts that bring us joy and serenity, as well as those that cause us stress and suffering. With consistent practice, we can become masters at navigating the streams of the mind.

## Beyond Duality

While exploring the duality of mind and consciousness, we may also discover that this duality actually dissolves. The mind and consciousness, although they may seem like two separate entities, are deeply interconnected. The moment we become aware of our thoughts, the mind itself becomes the object of consciousness's observation. In this sense, mind and consciousness merge into a single experience of self-observation.

*Conclusions*

The duality of mind and consciousness is one of the most fascinating mysteries of the human condition. It is an eternal dance between the creation of thoughts and their observation. This duality offers us the opportunity to choose how to respond to our thoughts and emotions, leading to inner freedom and personal growth.

In the following chapter, we will delve into the analysis of psychic entropy, investigating the nature of variations and fluctuations in the mental sphere. However, for now, let us take a moment to contemplate the extraordinary duality between the mind and consciousness and the potential to lead a more conscious and genuine life through its full understanding.

## CHAPTER 2: MENTAL ENTROPY

## THE NATURE OF CHANGES AND FLUCTUATIONS IN THE MIND.

On the journey toward a deeper understanding of the human mind, we encounter a constant and mysterious force that manifests in various subtle ways: mental entropy. This concept, borrowed from thermodynamics and adapted to the inner world of human beings, provides us with an illuminating perspective on the nature of changes and fluctuations in the mind.

*Entropy as a Measure of Disorder*

To fully grasp mental entropy, we must first examine its physical counterpart, thermodynamic entropy. In physics, entropy is a measure of a system's disorder. The higher the entropy, the more disordered and chaotic the system is. It's a fundamental principle of thermodynamics, stating that the entropy of a closed system always tends to increase over time. Paradoxically, this principle can be applied to our minds. The human mind is a complex and dynamic system, and here too, entropy can be viewed as a measure of mental disorder. When our mind is in a state of high entropy, we are often overwhelmed by a jumble of thoughts, emotions, and sensations, unable to find clarity or direction.

*Changes as Fluctuations in Entropy*

Changes in the mind are essentially fluctuations in mental entropy. When we face new experiences, acquire new information, or go through transitional moments in life, our mind adapts and changes. These changes are like fluctuations in entropy, shifting the mind between states of order and disorder. Imagine going through a significant life transition, such as changing jobs or relationships. Initially, the mind may find itself in a state of turbulence, with conflicting thoughts, doubts, and uncertainties. This is a phase of high mental entropy, where disorder reigns supreme. However, as time passes and reflection takes place, the mind begins to find a new equilibrium. The initial chaos transforms into renewed order, and confusion dissolves into a clearer understanding of the situation. Mental entropy decreases, and the mind regains its stability.

*Resistance to Change and Mental Entropy*

It's worth noting that not everyone embraces change with the same ease. Some individuals are more resistant to change, while others embrace the ebb and flow of mental fluctuations with an open attitude. Resistance to change can often be associated with a temporary increase in mental entropy. Imagine being deeply rooted in a routine or thought pattern that has served you well for years. When you encounter a situation that challenges this established pattern, your mind might initially react with confusion and disorder. Mental entropy increases as you try to adapt to the new reality.

However, with time and effort, the mind can gradually reduce entropy, finding a new equilibrium that incorporates the new experience. In this way, resistance to change can become an opportunity for personal growth and the evolution of the mind.

## Mental Entropy and Creativity

One fascinating aspect of mental entropy is its connection to creativity. In moments of high mental entropy, when the mind is suspended between chaos and order, spaces open up for innovation and creativity. It is during these phases that the mind is most open to new ideas and perspectives.

Think of the great artists, writers, and innovators in history. Many of them went through periods of deep mental turmoil before creating works that revolutionized the world. These moments of high mental entropy can be seen as preparatory phases for the birth of something new and astonishing.

## Changes as Opportunities for Growth

Mental entropy and changes in the mind should not be feared or avoided but rather embraced as opportunities for growth and learning. When we understand that change is an intrinsic part of human nature, we can embrace it with an attitude of openness and curiosity.

The next time you find yourself experiencing a period of change or fluctuation in your mind, consider embracing mental entropy as an ally rather than an enemy. This is the natural dance of the mind, the constant ebb and flow of inner waters that make us human.

## Conclusions

In the chapter on the "Nature of Changes and Fluctuations in the Mind," we explored mental entropy as a dynamic force that influences how we perceive and deal with changes in our lives. We saw how changes can be interpreted as fluctuations in mental entropy, shifting the mind between states of order and disorder.

Mental entropy should not be feared but understood as an integral part of the human experience. It is through the ebb and flow of mental change that we can grow, learn, and discover new perspectives.

In the following pages, we will delve further into the concept of mental entropy and explore the importance of addressing it for our well-being and personal growth. Continue to explore the flow of your reflections and thoughts as you immerse yourself in this journey of introspection.

# THE IMPORTANCE OF ADDRESSING MENTAL ENTROPY FOR WELL-BEING AND GROWTH

In our journey toward a deeper understanding of the human mind, we encounter an important reality: mental entropy. This subtle yet omnipresent force, as we saw in the previous chapter, is responsible for fluctuations in our minds, shifting them between states of order and disorder. But what is the significance of addressing mental entropy for our well-being and personal growth?

*Entropy as Challenge and Opportunity*

Confronting mental entropy is a challenge, but it is also an opportunity. When we find ourselves in a state of high mental entropy, we often experience confusion, anxiety, and uncertainty. Thoughts may seem out of control, and emotions can be overwhelming. This is the difficult part.

However, it is precisely in these challenging moments that the opportunity to grow and learn lies. When in a state of high entropy, we are forced to explore new perspectives and adapt to evolving circumstances. It's like navigating a stormy sea, where we learn to become more skilled navigators.

*Resistance to Entropy*

One of the primary challenges in addressing mental entropy is our natural resistance to change and disorder. The mind tends to cling to established and familiar thought patterns, even if these patterns no longer serve our well-being.

Imagine having a mental box in which you've accumulated beliefs, expectations, and habits over the years. This box represents a certain degree of mental order. When a new idea or situation arrives that challenges what's inside the box, the mind may initially resist. This resistance is a natural reflex.

However, it's important to recognize that resistance to mental entropy can become a barrier to our well-being and personal growth. When we rigidly cling to our mental patterns, we can remain trapped in situations that cause us stress and suffering.

*Mental Flexibility as the Key*

To address mental entropy constructively, it's essential to develop mental flexibility. Mental flexibility is the ability to adapt to new situations, embrace new perspectives, and let go of old thought patterns when they are no longer useful.

Imagine being a rock climber on a rock wall. Mental flexibility is like an elastic rope that allows you to move agilely from one grip to another. Without this flexibility, you might get stuck on a grip, unable to progress.

A concrete example of mental flexibility is the practice of mindfulness. During mindfulness, we learn to observe our thoughts and emotions without judgment. This practice helps us develop awareness of our mental patterns and be more open to new perspectives.

## Mental Entropy as a Driver of Growth

Mental entropy can also be seen as a driver of personal growth. When the mind is in a state of disorder, we are compelled to seek solutions and explore new paths. This process can lead to greater resilience and adaptability.

Imagine being a gardener working in a garden. Mental entropy is like a sudden storm that disrupts your garden. Initially, you might be dismayed by the devastation. But as you begin to repair and plant new seeds, your garden may ultimately become more lush and varied than before.

In a mental context, when we face the challenges of mental entropy, we can discover inner resources and qualities we didn't know we had. This is the beauty of personal growth.

## Managing Mental Entropy

Effectively addressing mental entropy requires active management. One of the key strategies for managing mental entropy is mindfulness. Becoming aware of our thoughts, emotions, and reactions is the first step in dealing with mental disorder.

Another important strategy is reflection. Taking the time to reflect on what we are experiencing and trying to find meaning in our experiences can help us navigate through mental entropy more constructively.

## Conclusions

Addressing mental entropy is an essential part of our journey towards growth and well-being. It's a challenge that requires us to develop mental flexibility, embrace change, and learn to manage inner disorder.

In the next chapter, we will explore the concept of "Vibrational Resonance" and how our inner vibrations can influence our mental and emotional state. Continue to explore this journey of self-analysis and personal growth as you delve deeper into the intricacies of the human mind.

# CHAPTER 3: VIBRATIONAL RESONANCE

## EXPLORING THE CONCEPT OF VIBRATIONAL RESONANCE IN THE SPIRIT

In our journey of exploring the mind and the human essence, we encounter an intriguing and mysterious concept: vibrational resonance. This concept goes beyond sensory perception and delves into the depths of our being, the subtle interconnection between spirit and the universe. In this chapter, we will delve into the depths of this vibrational resonance and seek to understand its profound significance.

*The Universe as an Orchestra of Vibrations*

To fully comprehend vibrational resonance, we must begin by exploring the very nature of the universe. According to quantum physics, everything that exists is composed of subatomic particles in constant motion. These particles vibrate at different frequencies and ultimately create what we perceive as matter and energy. Imagine the universe as an immense symphony orchestra where each particle is like a musician playing their instrument. Each instrument emits a note, and these notes blend to create a cosmic harmony. This is the foundation of vibrational resonance.

*Vibration as the Universal Language*

Vibrational resonance is a universal language that transcends cultural and linguistic barriers. It is the language through which the universe communicates with itself. Vibrations carry information, energy, and intentions.

Imagine being in a room with people from different languages. Even if you don't understand the words they say, you can perceive the energy of their vibrations, the tone of their voices, and the language of their bodies. It is through this subtle vibrational communication that we can understand the emotions of others, even without words.

## Our Personal Vibration

Every human being emits a unique vibration. This vibration is influenced by our thoughts, emotions, beliefs, and intentions. When we are in a state of happiness, love, and gratitude, our vibration is elevated and harmonious. In contrast, when dominated by fear, hatred, or negativity, our vibration becomes distorted and discordant.

Imagine being a musician playing an instrument in an orchestra. The quality of your performance influences the overall harmony of the orchestra. If you play with passion and mastery, you contribute to creating a harmonious melody. However, if you play disinterestedly or out of tune, you can disrupt the orchestra's harmony.

## The Law of Resonance

Vibrational resonance follows a fundamental law: "like attracts like." This means that vibrations with similar frequencies attract and reinforce each other. Imagine two musical notes that are in perfect harmony; they amplify each other, creating a richer and more powerful sound.

This law of resonance can be applied to our daily lives. If we want to attract positive experiences and harmonious relationships, we must emit corresponding vibrations. This requires inner work to raise our personal vibration through awareness, gratitude, and love.

*Vibration and Healing*

Vibrational resonance is also linked to healing. Some healing practices, such as traditional Chinese medicine and acupuncture, are based on the theory of subtle vibrations in the body. These practices seek to restore the harmony of vibrations to promote physical and mental healing.

Imagine the body as an orchestra with various instruments. When one instrument is out of tune or out of sync, the entire orchestra is affected. Similarly, when a part of our body or mind is in a state of disturbed vibration, it can negatively impact our overall health. Healing aims to reestablish the harmony of vibrations.

The Practice of Vibrational Awareness

One of the paths we can take to deepen our understanding of vibrational resonance is through the practice of vibrational awareness. This approach involves intentional and mindful attention to our inner vibrations, the emotions we experience, and the mental states we go through. This way, we move beyond mere recognition of emotions and thoughts, focusing instead on the perception of the vibrations underlying these experiences.

Here's how you can start:

1. *Vibrational Awareness Meditation:*

   Set aside time each day to meditate and focus on your inner vibrations. Sit in a quiet place, close your eyes, and direct your attention to the sensation of energy within your body. Observe how the vibrations of your emotions and thoughts manifest.

2. *Emotion Listening:*

   When you experience intense emotions, take a moment to listen to their vibration. Ask yourself how it manifests in your body. For example, joy might feel like a sense of lightness and openness, while fear might be experienced as contraction or tension. Observe these vibrations without judgment.

3. *Conscious Vibration Choices:*

   Once you have become aware of your inner vibrations, you can begin to make conscious choices to elevate them. Seek to cultivate thoughts of love, gratitude, and compassion. Engage in activities that make you feel in harmony with yourself and the universe.

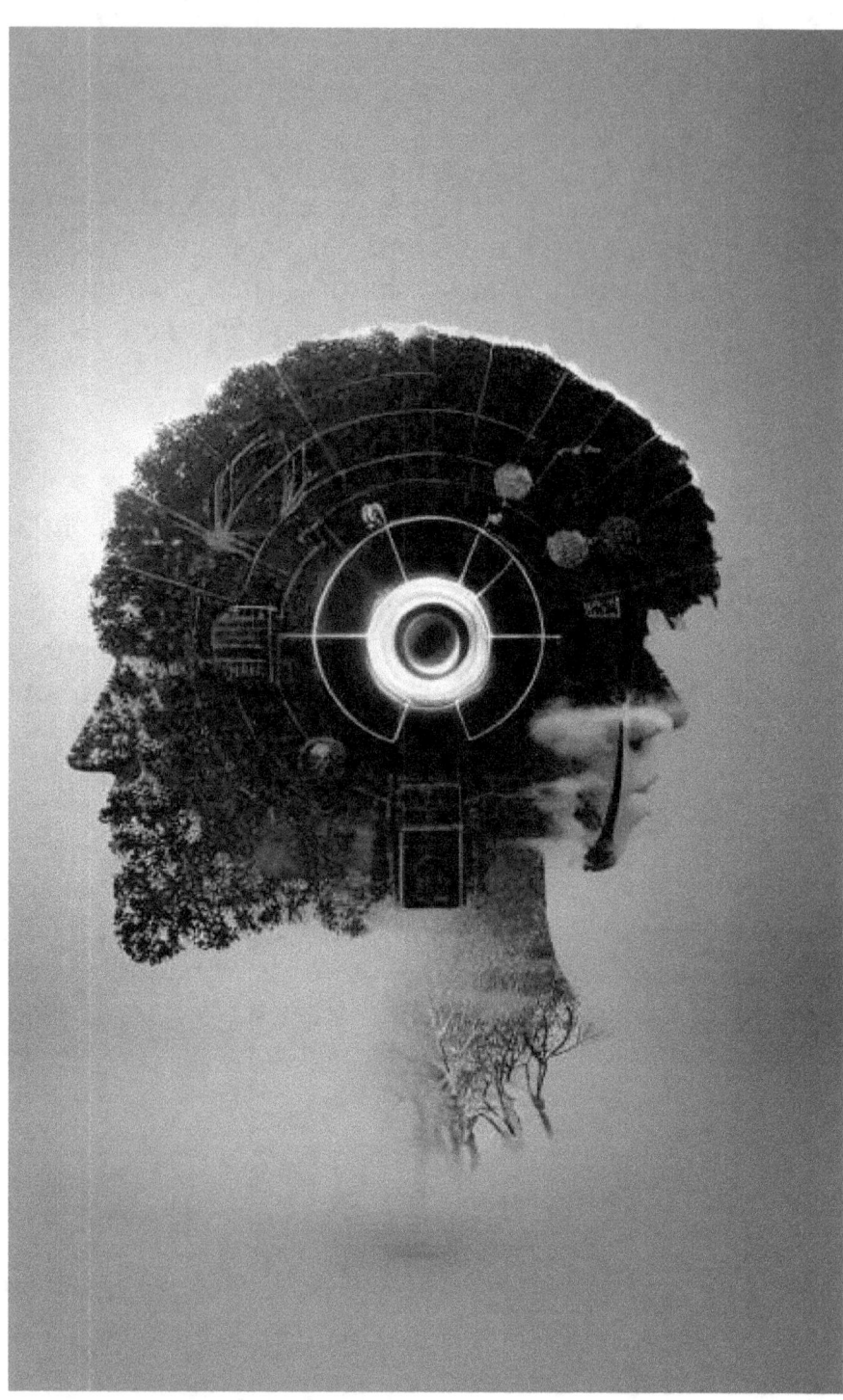

4. *Resonance with the Environment:*

Observe how your vibrational state influences your environment and the people around you. When you emit positive vibrations, you are more likely to attract positive experiences and relationships. This is a reflection of the law of resonance.

*Beyond the Duality of Mind-Consciousness:*

In the context of the duality of mind and consciousness that we explored in the previous chapter, vibrational resonance becomes a bridge between these two dimensions. The mind creates thoughts and emotions, which, in turn, generate vibrations. Consciousness observes these vibrations and can influence them through awareness.

Imagine the mind as a musician playing a melody and consciousness as a conductor. The conductor can guide the musician toward a harmonious or dissonant melody based on their awareness. Similarly, consciousness can influence the vibrations generated by the mind through its awareness and intention.

*Conclusions:*

Vibrational resonance is a fascinating concept that connects us to the very essence of the universe. It is a universal language that goes beyond words and allows us to communicate with the inner and outer world in deep and meaningful ways.

In the following chapters, we will explore the various architectures of the mind, the different layers of the subconscious that influence our vibrations and awareness. Continue on your journey of introspection and discovery, as each advancement brings us closer to understanding ourselves and the vast reality in which we are immersed.

# HOW OUR VIBRATIONS INFLUENCE OUR MENTAL AND EMOTIONAL STATE

In the inner silence of every individual, deep in the heart of being, vibrations dance like notes in an infinite symphony. These vibrations, often eluding conscious perception, are the very essence of our existence. In this chapter, we will explore how these vibrations can subtly yet powerfully influence our mental and emotional state.

## The Orchestra of Inner Vibrations

Imagine your mind and body as an orchestra, with every emotion, thought, and mood playing its part in the symphony of your inner vibrations. Like a conductor, your consciousness guides this symphony, influencing the tone and rhythm of the notes.

Vibrations can vary widely. There are vibrations of joy, love, serenity, but also vibrations of fear, anger, and sadness. Each emotion has its frequency, intensity, and melody. When we experience an emotion, we are actually perceiving a specific combination of these vibrations.

## The Interactive Cycle

The relationship between vibrations and our mental and emotional state is an interactive cycle. The emotions we feel generate specific vibrations, which, in turn, affect our mental state. If we feel happy, the vibrations of joy amplify our perception of happiness. Conversely, when we are sad, the vibrations of sadness can lower our mood.

The mind is also a key player in this cycle. Our thoughts can trigger emotions and, consequently, specific vibrations. For instance, thoughts of gratitude can generate vibrations of joy, while thoughts of worry may lead to vibrations of anxiety.

*The Science of Emotional Vibrations*

Modern science has started to examine this phenomenon. Studies in Emotional Intelligence and Positive Psychology have shown how positive emotions, and thus positive vibrations, are correlated with better mental and physical health.

Some researchers have also explored how vibrations influence our autonomic nervous system. Positive vibrations appear to favor the parasympathetic nervous system, associated with relaxation and well-being. Conversely, negative vibrations can activate the sympathetic nervous system, known for its involvement in the stress response.

*The Power of Awareness*

Awareness of these vibrations is the first step in consciously influencing them. When we become aware of the vibrations we are experiencing, we can intervene more effectively to change our mental and emotional state.

Here are some strategies to do this:

1. *Observation of Vibrations:*

   Dedicate time each day to reflect on your inner vibrations. Ask yourself how you feel and what vibrations you are experiencing. Recognizing your emotions is the first step in influencing them.

2. *State Change:*

   When you realize you are experiencing unwanted vibrations, you can consciously intervene to change them. For example, if you feel stressed, you can practice deep breathing to promote more relaxed vibrations.

3. *Cultivate Love and Gratitude:*

   Some of the most positive vibrations are associated with love and gratitude. Cultivate these emotions through practices like gratitude meditation or expressing love to others.

4. *Positive Mind:*

   Pay attention to your thoughts. If you notice negative thoughts generating unwanted vibrations, try to replace them with more positive and constructive thoughts

5. *Positive Sharing:*

   Vibrations can be shared. Spend time with positive people and share happy moments with others. This sharing can increase positive vibrations in a contagious manner.

## The Influence of the Environment

In addition to our personal vibrations, the environment around us can influence our vibrations. A harmonious environment with natural elements and relaxing colors can promote positive vibrations. Conversely, a chaotic and stressful environment can have a negative impact on our vibrations.

## Conclusion

Inner vibrations are an essential part of our human experience. Understanding how these vibrations influence our mental and emotional state offers us a powerful tool to improve our mental health and emotional well-being.

In the next chapter, we will embark on an in-depth journey into the analysis of the structures of the mind, examining the various depths of our subconscious that underlie the oscillations of our energy and our perception of them. It will be a detailed investigation of complex mental architectures, the stratifications that characterize our inner world, and shape our awareness.

# CHAPTER 4: MIND ARCHITECTURES

In the mysterious theater of our mind, there exist intricate and fascinating mechanisms that govern our experience and perceptions. In this chapter, we will delve into the depths of the human mind to explore its hidden architectures, the various layers of the subconscious that influence our consciousness and actions.

## The Foundations of the Unconscious

Imagine the mind as an iceberg, with only a small visible part above the water's surface and the majority hidden in the depths. The visible part represents our conscious mind, where our awareness and rational thinking reside. But beneath the surface lies the vast world of the unconscious.

The unconscious is like a repository of memories, emotions, and past experiences. It is where our repressed desires, buried fears, and deep-seated beliefs reside. These elements can exert a considerable influence on our conscious life, often in ways we don't fully understand.

## The Unconscious and Dreams

A window into the unconscious opens when we dream. Dreams are like the theater of the unconscious, where symbolic dramas and cryptic scenes unfold. Psychoanalysts like Sigmund Freud have suggested that dreams are a way to explore the contents of the unconscious and reveal hidden desires and conflicts.
However, dreams can be enigmatic and challenging to interpret. Jung, a student of Freud, further developed this

theory, suggesting that dreams contain symbols and archetypes that reflect the depths of humanity's collective unconscious.

## The Power of Habits and Conditioning

Much of our daily actions are guided by habits and conditioning residing in the unconscious. For instance, when we drive a car, much of this activity is automated, thanks to driving patterns we've learned over the years. These patterns are stored in the unconscious and allow us to perform complex actions with little or no conscious awareness.

However, this automatism can also be a trap. Often, habits and conditioning in the unconscious lead us to react automatically to situations that would require a more reflective response. Becoming aware of these dynamics is essential for our personal development.

## The Creative Subconscious

Despite the unconscious appearing as a dark and mysterious place, it is also the source of inspiration and creativity. Many artists, writers, and inventors have claimed that their most creative ideas emerge from the unconscious. This aspect of the subconscious is often referred to as the "creative subconscious."

When we allow the conscious mind to relax, the unconscious can emerge with inventive solutions and profound insights. This is why many people find inspiration in the shower or during a walk. By letting the conscious mind loosen its grip, we allow the creative subconscious to flourish.

## The Invisible Architectures

The architectures of the mind are like an underground city of which we are barely aware. However, becoming aware of these depths can open up new perspectives on our life and well-being.

Practices like meditation, for instance, help us delve into the depths of the mind and explore the unconscious. Self-awareness, psychological therapy, and other personal development techniques can also help us unveil the secrets of the unconscious. Exploring the architectures of the mind takes us into uncharted territory where the unconscious and the subconscious act in mysterious and powerful ways. Understanding these hidden layers of the mind can provide a key to our personal and spiritual development.

## The Universal Mind: The Interweaving of Being

In our journey through the complex architectures of the mind, we arrive at a fascinating and profound concept: the Universal Mind. This concept suggests that our individual mind is interconnected with the entire consciousness of the universe, a perspective that challenges our traditional understanding of the mind and reality itself.

*Cosmic Interweaving*

Imagine the individual mind as a drop of water in the ocean of the Universe. While appearing separate, the drop is intrinsically connected to the ocean from which it comes. The Universal Mind suggests that every individual mind is part of a broader intelligence, a collective consciousness permeating all of existence.

This concept is not new. Ancient spiritual traditions such as Vedanta in India or the concept of the "World Soul" in Greek philosophy have suggested a form of the Universal Mind. This view implies that every form of life, every thought, and every emotion are part of a cosmic interweaving, contributing to the fabric of the universe itself.

*Theory of Consciousness Waves*

To better understand the Universal Mind, we can explore the theory of consciousness waves. This theory suggests that our individual minds are like radio stations tuning into specific frequencies within a vast network of consciousness waves.
Each frequency represents a different mental or emotional state. When we tune our minds to a specific frequency, we perceive the world accordingly. For example, anger and love could be perceived as two different radio stations, each tuned to a unique frequency.

This theory suggests that our individual mind plays an active part in creating our reality. When we change our mental frequency, we experience the world in different ways. This explains why the same situation can be perceived very differently from one individual to another.

*Sharing Universal Experiences*

An intriguing aspect of the Universal Mind is the sharing of universal experiences. This concept suggests that profound and meaningful experiences, such as love, beauty, mystery, and connection, are not individual experiences but rather manifestations of a collective consciousness.

When we experience the beauty of a sunset, for instance, it is not only our individual mind perceiving that beauty, but the Universal Mind itself expressing through us. This can explain why such profound experiences have the power to connect us to a sense of unity with the world and with other human beings.

*The Universal Mind and the Transcendence of the Individual*

Understanding the Universal Mind has profound implications for our view of ourselves as individuals. It suggests that our identity is not limited to the boundaries of the individual mind but encompasses a broader dimension of universal consciousness.
This perspective can lead us to greater compassion and a sense of responsibility toward humanity and the environment. We realize that our actions are not isolated but contribute to the very fabric of universal consciousness. The consequences of our actions extend far beyond our individual selves.

## The Practice of Cosmic Connection

To explore and experience the Universal Mind, we can adopt spiritual and meditative practices that help us connect with this broader dimension of consciousness. Meditation, in particular, can allow us to transcend the limits of the individual mind and experience moments of unity with the cosmos.

In these states of cosmic connection, we may discover a sense of deep peace, understanding, and universal love. This can enrich our daily lives, bringing us to a new level of awareness and respect for all forms of life.

## Conclusions

The Universal Mind is a profound and fascinating concept that urges us to explore the hidden architectures of the human mind. This perspective challenges us to look beyond the boundaries of our individual mind and recognize our connection to the entire consciousness of the universe. In the pages that follow, we will delve into the investigation of the multiple layers that constitute the mind and the subconscious. This path of exploration will lead us toward a deeper understanding of who we are and our role within the existential context, as every progress we make brings us closer to this enlightenment.

# EXPLORING THE VARIOUS LAYERS OF THE MIND AND THE SUBCONSCIOUS.

In our journey of uncovering the architectures of the mind, let's delve into the various layers that constitute our inner world. The human mind is like an iceberg, with much of its processes hidden beneath the surface of consciousness. Each layer reveals a different aspect of our psyche, each with its role and influence on our daily experiences.

*The Conscious Mind: The Surface of the Iceberg*

Let's begin with the conscious mind, the part of the iceberg that emerges above the water's surface. This layer represents our daytime awareness, the place where we make decisions, process information, and are mindful of our sensory experiences. It's the mind we use to navigate daily life.

However, the conscious mind is just the tip of the iceberg. Its capacity to process information is limited, and much of our thinking and decision-making is influenced by deeper and less accessible layers of the mind.

*The Subconscious: Depths Below the Surface*

Descending beneath the surface, we enter the realm of the subconscious. This layer contains information and experiences that are not immediately accessible to the conscious mind but play a significant role in our psyche.

The subconscious stores memories, beliefs, fears, and desires that can influence our thoughts, emotions, and behavior without our awareness. For instance, a traumatic childhood experience can leave an imprint in the subconscious, influencing how we react to similar situations even years later.

*The Unconscious: The Deepest Depths*

Even deeper still, we find the unconscious, the most mysterious and inaccessible part of the mind. This layer contains primal instincts, drives, repressed desires, and archetypal forces that shape much of our behavior.

The unconscious can surface in dreams, slips of the tongue, and symbols that appear in our daily life. Jung described it as a vast reservoir of images and symbols, a place where our experiences and the experiences of humanity are shared and stored.

*Cellular Memories and Heredity*

In addition to the subconscious and unconscious, there is another layer of the mind that is less explored but equally influential: cellular memories and heredity. Modern science has shown that the experiences of our ancestors can influence our DNA and be passed down through generations.

This means that memories of our family roots, the traumas or joys of our ancestors, can resonate within us, even if we are not consciously aware of them. This complex interplay between heredity and personal memory can contribute to shaping our behavior and reactions to life's events.

*Exploring the Deep Layers*

Exploring the various layers of the mind is a fascinating and challenging journey. It requires self-reflection, introspection, and sometimes the help of mental health professionals to unveil the mysteries hidden in the depths of the human psyche.

Understanding these deep layers can lead to greater self-awareness, enabling us to break free from limiting thought patterns and resolve inner traumas and conflicts. This can significantly contribute to our psychological well-being and personal growth.

*Integrating the Levels of the Mind*

The art of self-understanding and personal transformation lies in the integration of these various levels of the mind. We cannot simply explore one layer without considering the others. Self-awareness requires delving deep into the recesses of the human psyche, bringing to light those thoughts and feelings that can subtly but significantly influence our lives.

*The Integration Process*

Integration is not a simple process. It requires time, patience, and ongoing self-reflection. Here are some key phases in the process of integrating the various layers of the mind:

1. *Awareness:*

The first step is becoming aware of these layers of the mind. It's necessary to acknowledge that the mind is not a single uniform layer but a complex interconnection of levels.

2. *Exploration:*

Once awareness is gained, it's time to explore the different layers. This can involve self-reflection, meditation, working with a therapist, or journaling to deepen self-understanding.

3. *Acceptance:*

Each layer of the mind may contain challenging elements, such as painful memories or deep-seated fears. Integration requires accepting these aspects without judgment or resistance. Acceptance is the first step toward transformation.

4. *Connection:*

After you've begun to explore and accept these layers, try to connect them to one another. Find the links between your memories, emotions, and beliefs. Recognize how they mutually influence your thinking and behavior.

5. *Transformation:*

Integration is not just an act of recognition but also one of transformation. When you integrate the various layers of the mind, you can work on changing them positively. This might involve revising your limiting beliefs, overcoming past traumas, or enhancing your inner resources.

6. *Ongoing Awareness:*

Integration is an ongoing process. The mind is fluid and ever-evolving, so your awareness and integration work should be equally dynamic. Keep exploring, connecting, and transforming the various layers of the mind throughout your life.

*The Benefits of Integration*

Integrating the various layers of the mind can lead to numerous benefits. It can help you overcome limiting thought patterns, free yourself from past traumas, and improve your self-understanding. This process can promote greater emotional stability, better stress management, and increased resilience in life's challenges.

Moreover, it can lead to greater awareness of how your thoughts and emotions influence your behavior and relationships. This awareness can enhance the quality of your interactions with others and lead to a more authentic and meaningful life.

*Conclusions*

The exploration and integration of the multiple layers of the mind constitute a crucial element of the journey of self-understanding and personal development. This endeavor can prove to be profound and challenging but offers extraordinary opportunities for growth, evolution, and leading a more conscious and rewarding life. Persisting in the search of these intricate mental structures plays a fundamental role as each step of progress gradually leads to a deeper understanding of one's authentic essence.

# THE IMPORTANCE OF UNDERSTANDING MENTAL STRUCTURES TO TRANSFORM LIMITING THOUGHT PATTERNS.

Within the vast universe of the human mind, intricate labyrinths of mental structures are hidden, and although invisible to the eye, they have a surprisingly tangible impact on our daily lives. These structures form the foundation of our thought patterns, and understanding their functioning is crucial to free ourselves from those limiting thoughts that often imprison us.

*Mental Structures as Hidden Architectures*

Imagine mental structures as the foundations of a house. They are hidden underground, invisible to the eye, but they support everything above them. Similarly, mental structures form the basis upon which our thought patterns rest. These structures include beliefs, thought patterns, perceptions, and judgments that we often take for granted.

For example, you may have a deeply ingrained mental structure that leads you to believe that you are not capable or do not deserve success. This belief may stem from past experiences, cultural influences, or even teachings received in early life. This structure, if not recognized and understood, can continue to shape your thinking in ways that limit your opportunities and well-being.

*The Art of Awareness*

The first step in transforming limiting thought patterns is becoming aware of the mental structures that underpin them. This requires a courageous and honest act of introspection. It's like embarking on a journey into the darkness to explore the foundations of your mind.

Awareness is the light that illuminates these hidden structures. It's the power to look within yourself with an objective and non-judgmental eye. When you begin to recognize the beliefs and patterns you've inherited or created over the years, you can question them.

*The Power of Research and Analysis*

Once you've gained awareness of your mental structures, you can begin to explore them deeply. Ask yourself where they come from. Are they the result of past experiences? Have they been influenced by the culture or environment in which you grew up? These questions can reveal the invisible threads that hold these structures together.

Here's an example: you may have a limiting belief about your ability to make important decisions. Perhaps you've experienced a significant failure in the past, and now you believe you are not capable of making wise choices. This is a mental structure that will influence your present decisions unless you examine it closely. Once you've identified the origin of this belief, you can begin to challenge it.

## Transformation Through Awareness

Transforming limiting thought patterns requires time and commitment. It must be a process guided by continuous awareness and the will to change. This does not mean denying the past or avoiding negative thoughts, but rather acknowledging them and choosing not to be enslaved by them. One of the most powerful techniques for transforming mental structures is cognitive reframing. This involves rethinking limiting beliefs in more positive and constructive ways. For example, you can transform the thought "I am unable to make decisions" into "I can learn from mistakes and make wise decisions."

## Living a Mindful Life

As you become increasingly aware of your mental structures and the thought patterns that guide your life, you begin to see new opportunities. Life ceases to be governed by limiting beliefs, and new possibilities start to emerge. This is the point where real transformation can occur. You can begin to experience a life based on mindfulness rather than automatic reactions to old mental patterns. For example, if you've always had low self-esteem due to criticism received in your youth, by becoming aware of this mental structure, you can start working on building a new self-esteem. You can adopt practices that promote self-confidence, such as self-compassion, self-affirmation, and celebrating your successes.

## A Practical Example

To illustrate how understanding mental structures can lead to positive transformation, consider the example of Maria.

Maria has always believed she's not a creative person due to a critical comment from a teacher when she was a child. This limiting belief led her to avoid creative activities throughout her life. However, when Maria embarks on a journey of self-exploration and becomes aware of her limiting mental structure, she decides to challenge it. She starts attending art classes and engaging in creative projects. Eventually, she discovers that she has a natural talent for art, and her creativity was merely suppressed by limiting beliefs. This example demonstrates how awareness of mental structures can lead to significant transformation in a person's life. Maria learned to overcome a limiting belief and embraced a part of herself that had long been suppressed.

*Conclusion*

Understanding mental structures is crucial to free ourselves from the limiting thought patterns that often imprison us. This process requires self-awareness, research, and the courage to challenge the beliefs that hold us back. But through this transformation, we can open new doors to a life based on mindfulness, authenticity, and personal growth.

In the next chapter, we will explore the concept of intuition and how it can be cultivated to make wiser decisions and connect with the inner world. Continue your journey of discovery into the human mind, as the depths of the human psyche are infinite and ever-evolving.

# INTUITION

In the vast landscape of the human mind, intuition represents a precious gem. It is that silent voice that whispers wisdom in moments of uncertainty, an inner guide that helps us make wiser decisions and connect with the deep world of our consciousness.

## The Nature of Intuition

Before delving into the art of cultivating intuition, it is essential to understand its intrinsic nature. Intuition is not a product of rational thought or logic; instead, it emerges from our inner world, from the vast ocean of the subconscious. It is like a reflection of our past experiences, deep values, and subtle perceptions.

Often, intuition manifests as visceral sensations, small flashes of inspiration, or a sudden sense of certainty. It cannot be forced or summoned at will; it must flow naturally. However, we can train ourselves to become more aware of these intuitive manifestations and listen to them attentively.

## Intuition and Wise Decisions

One of the most common challenges in life is decision-making. Faced with crossroads and intersections, we often seek answers in rationality and detailed analysis. However, intuition offers another perspective. What may seem like a "stroke of luck" or a "gut feeling" can actually be intuition emerging to guide us.

Imagine being at a significant decision point, such as a career choice or a relationship decision. Instead of relying solely on pros and cons, you can pause and seek that subtle inner voice. What does intuition suggest? What is the feeling that guides you in one direction rather than another?

*Intuition as a Life Companion*

Intuition can become a valuable life companion. When we cultivate it and learn to listen, it can accompany us in many aspects of our existence. This inner guidance can help us not only in important decisions but also in understanding our deepest desires and needs.

In everyday life, we can experience intuition as a "sense" that suggests we do something or avoid something else. For example, you might have the intuition to take a walk in the park, and as you do, you might meet someone who will have a significant impact on your life. These moments are often the result of listening to intuition.

*Cultivating Intuition*

But how can we cultivate this precious inner resource? The practice of meditation is a powerful tool for developing awareness and attention to intuitive signals. During meditation, we learn to quiet the mind and create a space for intuition to emerge.

Furthermore, keeping an intuition journal can be helpful. Each time you experience an intuitive moment, make a note of it. What were you doing? What did you feel? What did you perceive? This can help you identify patterns and trends in your intuitions.

*Intuition and Inner Connection*

Lastly, intuition is closely tied to our connection with the inner world. When we connect with our deepest values, authentic desires, and fears, we become more receptive to intuitions that emerge in response to such connections.

In conclusion, intuition is a valuable resource residing within us. Cultivating and listening to it can lead to wiser decisions and a deeper connection with ourselves. In the next chapter, we will further explore the connection between intuition and the inner world, opening the door to greater self-awareness and personal growth.

*Intuition and Inner Connection: A Profound Relationship*

Intuition is like a bridge between our inner world and the external reality. When we are attuned to our inner world, we become more open to emerging intuitions. This process requires a profound connection with ourselves.

One of the keys to further developing this connection is the practice of mindfulness. Self-awareness means being present in the moment, acknowledging our thoughts, emotions, and sensations without judgment. Mindfulness helps us discover who we truly are beyond social masks and external expectations.

## Intuition as a Guide for Life's Journey

Often, the most significant decisions in life pertain to who we want to be and what we want to achieve. Here, intuition can become a reliable guide. When we are connected to our inner world, we become more attentive to intuitive signals that point the way.

Imagine standing at a career crossroads. You feel that subtle sensation, that small inner voice urging you to pursue a certain path. This is the power of intuition in action. It's like an internal map that can help us navigate life's complex choices.

## Listening to Intuition in Relationships

Intuition is valuable not only for personal decisions but also for relationships. When we are connected to our inner world, we become more sensitive to intuitive signals within relational dynamics.

For example, you might sense a slight discomfort in the presence of a person, even if you can't identify an apparent reason. This intuitive feeling could be a call to attention to hidden dynamics or values incompatibility.

## Intuition as a Response to the Unknown

Life is often a series of unknowns, and intuition can be our internal compass for addressing them. When we face complex or ambiguous situations, intuition can offer a guiding light.

Imagine being confronted with a decision involving apparent risk. Logic may tell you to avoid the risk, but intuition might suggest embracing it. This challenge of uncertainty is where intuition can shine, pushing us beyond our comfort zones.

## Intuition as a Key to Personal Growth

Cultivating intuition is also a path to personal growth. It requires a consistent practice of self-reflection, self-observation, and mindfulness. Gradually, we become more skilled at discerning the true voices of intuition from the distortions of fear or desire.

Intuition can also lead us to greater empathy and understanding of others. When we are tuned into our inner world, we become more capable of sensing the emotions and needs of others, which can enrich our relationships and our ability to support others.

## Conclusion: Intuition as Life's Navigator

In conclusion, intuition is a hidden treasure within us. It is a valuable resource for making wise decisions, nurturing meaningful relationships, and pursuing a path of personal growth. To tune into our intuition, we must establish a deep connection with our inner world, relying on our acute awareness and dedicating time to self-reflection. This process involves a deep immersion into the dimension of our inner selves, allowing us to align our perception with the intuitive flow that pervades our existence.

# CHAPTER 5: EXPLORING THE SOUL

The essence of humanity is not confined within the walls of the brain or the barriers of the physical body; it extends into the infinite realm of the soul. The soul is the vibrant core that permeates every aspect of our existence. In this chapter, we will immerse ourselves in the dark and mysterious depths of the soul, exploring its contours and learning to understand its hidden wisdom.

## The Soul: An Endless Mystery

The soul is a concept rich in meaning and mystery. It has been described in many religious, philosophical, and spiritual traditions as the immaterial and eternal part of the human being. While the mind and body may wither over time, the soul is considered eternal, a divine spark that connects each of us to the universe itself.

## The Soul as a Mirror of Experience

The soul is also seen as the guardian of our experience. Every emotion, every thought, every interaction we have in life is imprinted on the soul. It's like a vast mirror that reflects our experiences, collecting and safeguarding them with care.

Imagine the soul as an ancient manuscript that records every word, every thought, every act of your life. This record is not made of ink and paper but of energy and awareness. It's a record of your deepest emotions, your moments of joy and sadness, your hopes, and your fears.

## The Journey to the Soul

To understand the soul, we must embark on an inner journey. It is a journey that requires courage, self-reflection, and an open mind. Many spiritual traditions teach that the soul can only be understood through self-inquiry and deep contemplation.

The first step on this journey is self-awareness. We must learn to look beyond social masks and superficial identities to discover who we truly are. This requires sincerity and honesty with ourselves, a willingness to explore the shadows and lights of our being.

## The Soul and Its Dark Depths

In our journey to the soul, we often encounter its dark depths. The soul is not just light and love; it also contains the shadows, traumas, and conflicts we have experienced in our lives. Exploring these dark depths is an essential part of the soul's journey.

The shadows of the soul represent the parts of ourselves that we have hidden or removed from our consciousness. They are repressed emotions, unhealed wounds, and aspects of ourselves that we have refused to accept. These shadows can influence our actions and choices in subtle but powerful ways.

## The Soul as a Source of Inspiration and Creativity

The soul is also an infinite source of inspiration and creativity. When we open ourselves to the soul, we allow this creative energy to flow through us. This can manifest in various ways: through art, music, writing, or simply through the joy of living.

When we create from a place of connection with the soul, our artistic expressions become authentic and meaningful. We can convey deep emotions and thoughts, striking chords of humanity that resonate in all of us. Art that flows from the soul has the power to inspire, heal, and transform both the artist and anyone who comes into contact with it.

*The Soul as a Bridge between the Individual and the Universal*

The soul is also seen as the bridge between the individual and the universal. While it represents our uniqueness and personal experience, it is also connected to something larger than ourselves. Some call it the Higher Self, while others define it as a connection to all of humanity or cosmic energy.

In moments of deep meditation or contemplation, we can experience this connection with the universal. We feel like a part of a greater whole, in harmony with the entire cosmos. This experience of unity can lead to a sense of peace, understanding, and profound acceptance.

*Cultivating the Connection with the Soul*

Cultivating a connection with the soul takes time and practice.

Here are some paths to begin the journey:

**1.** *Meditation and Contemplation*

Meditation is a powerful way to quiet the mind, center ourselves, and connect with the soul. During meditation, we can let shallow thoughts dissolve and listen to the deeper voices of the soul. Contemplation, on the other hand, allows us to reflect on profound questions and explore the meaning of life.

**2.** Creativity and Artistic Expression

Exploring creativity through art, writing, dance, or any other form of artistic expression can help unleash the energy of the soul. When we create from the soul, we connect with a flow of inspiration that goes beyond rational thought.

**3.** *Community and Sharing*

Sharing experiences with others can be a powerful source of soul connection. In supportive communities, we can find understanding, empathy, and shared experiences. This sharing can strengthen the sense of spiritual connection.

**4.** *Nature and Mindfulness*

Spending time in nature and practicing mindfulness can help tune in to the soul. The beauty of nature and the stillness of the mind can open the door to deep contemplation and inner connection.

## The Soul as an Inner Guide

The concept of a soul as a guide in our lives is fascinating and deeply meaningful. In this chapter, we will further explore the idea of a soul as a guide and how we can tune into it to find direction, wisdom, and inspiration in our lives.

## The Silent Voice of the Soul

The soul speaks in a silent language, yet its voice can be powerful. It is the underlying feeling that tells us what is right or wrong, guides us in important decisions, and propels us toward what truly impassions us. Often, the soul's voice is drowned out by the noise of the external world and the incessant chatter of the mind. However, it is always there, ready to be heard.

## Listening to the Soul

Listening to the soul requires an act of inner silence. It means slowing down enough to hear the deep voice that lies behind the daily clamor. One way to do this is through meditation. During meditation, we create space in our minds to allow the soul to emerge and communicate clearly.

But soul-listening is not limited to meditation. We can practice active listening in moments of quiet and reflection. We can ask ourselves deep questions and give voice to our most authentic thoughts. We can observe the emotions that arise and ask ourselves what they are trying to tell us.

*Tuning into the Soul*

Tuning into the soul is like adjusting a radio to receive a clear station. It requires patience and attention. Here are some ways to do it:

**1.** *Practice Mindfulness*

Mindfulness is crucial for tuning into the soul. It means being present in the moment, carefully observing our thoughts and emotions, and listening to what they tell us. Mindfulness helps us separate from mental noise and get closer to the soul's voice.

**2.** *Follow Your Passion*

The soul often speaks through passion. What deeply impassions us is often a reflection of the soul's most authentic desires. Following your passion can be a way to honor and listen to your inner guidance.

**3.** *Make Room for Creativity*

The soul finds expression in creativity. Writing, painting, dancing, playing music, or engaging in any form of artistic expression can help give voice to the soul. Creativity is a channel through which the soul communicates.

**4.** *Ask Deep Questions*

Pose deep questions to yourself and listen to the answers that emerge. These answers may come from the soul and provide valuable guidance on your life and the choices you need to make.

## The Soul as a Guide to a Meaningful Life

When we listen to the soul and tune into its guidance, we tend to live more meaningful and fulfilling lives. The soul knows our deepest purpose, our true passions, and what truly makes us happy. By following this inner guidance, we can make choices that resonate with who we truly are and bring more joy into our lives.

But soul-listening requires courage. It means being willing to challenge the expectations of others, make difficult decisions, and embrace our authenticity. However, the reward is a life lived in harmony with oneself, a life that truly reflects who we are.

# ACCESSING THE DEPTHS OF THE HUMAN SOUL

In the previous chapter, we explored the concept of a soul as a guide in our lives and how we can tune into it for direction and wisdom. In this chapter, we will delve even deeper into the notion of the soul and venture into the depths of the human soul. We will seek to understand what lies within its depths, how to access these hidden dimensions, and what significance they may hold for our existence.

## The Soul as a Mirror of the Universe

Many philosophers and mystics have described the soul as a mirror of the universe. This means that within each of us, there is a reflection of what exists in the universe itself. The soul contains the totality of human and universal experience. It is the bridge between our inner world and the infinity of the universe. To access the depths of the human soul, we must understand that every aspect of our personal experience is reflected within it. Joys and sorrows, hopes and fears, dreams and disappointments, everything is archived in the soul. It is like an infinite library that holds every written page of our lives.

## Exploring the Unconscious

One of the keys to accessing the depths of the soul is the exploration of the unconscious. The unconscious is a dimension of the soul that lies beyond ordinary awareness. It is like the deep ocean we dive into when we seek to understand the hidden meaning of events, emotions, or dreams.

Depth psychology, including Jungian analysis and Freudian psychoanalysis, has sought to shed light on the human unconscious. These disciplines teach us that many of our actions and thoughts are driven by hidden forces within ourselves. Exploring the unconscious requires courage but can lead to a greater understanding of who we truly are.

## The Art of Introspection

Introspection is another path to accessing the depths of the soul. It means looking within oneself with honesty and without judgment. It is like embarking on a journey into the darkness of one's psyche, illuminating it with the light of awareness.

Meditation, journaling, and inner dialogue are useful tools for introspection. These practices allow us to explore our deepest thoughts, desires, and fears and highlight the connections between our past and present experiences.

## Confronting the Shadow

One of the most intriguing aspects of the soul is the concept of the shadow. The shadow represents all those aspects of ourselves that we tend to deny or repress. It is what we don't want to see in ourselves. However, confronting the shadow is essential for accessing the depths of the soul. Carl Jung, the famous Swiss psychologist, once said, "Anyone who has not made peace with their own shadow is destined to suffer." In other words, ignoring the dark aspects of ourselves can lead to inner conflicts and dissonance.

Confronting the shadow requires courage and self-compassion. It means taking a close look at our flaws, self-destructive behaviors, and the parts of ourselves we might wish to hide from others. But only through this acceptance can we hope to reach the depths of the soul.

*The Beauty of the Soul*

In the depths of the soul, we can also find beauty. The soul is like a precious jewel with many facets. It can reflect the light of joy, compassion, creativity, and human connection. When we access these dimensions of the soul, we can experience a beauty that transcends words.
The beauty of the soul can be revealed through art, music, nature, or any other experience that deeply touches us. When we are in tune with the soul, we can see beauty in everything, even in life's challenges and difficult moments.

Accessing the depths of the human soul is a lifelong journey. It's a path of self-discovery, an understanding of the complexity of the human being, and a connection with the universe itself. But it's a journey worth undertaking because in the depths of the soul, we can find meaning, wisdom, and beauty that enrich our existence.

In our journey through the depths of the human soul, we have explored the idea that the soul is like a mirror of the universe, an archive of our personal and universal experiences. Now, what remains to be discovered is how we can apply this understanding of the soul in our relationships with others and in our contributions to the world.

## Relationships as a Mirror of the Soul

Human relationships can be seen as a mirror of the soul. Every interaction with another person can reflect aspects of ourselves that might otherwise be hidden or inaccessible. When we engage in relationships with others, we confront their emotions, thoughts, and experiences, and this can lead us to explore parts of ourselves we may not have previously recognized.

For example, if we find ourselves in a conflictual relationship, we may be compelled to examine our tendencies towards anger or fear. On the other hand, if we immerse ourselves in a relationship based on love and mutual understanding, we may discover new depths of empathy and affection within ourselves.

## Empathy and Soul Connection

A deeper understanding of the soul can lead to increased empathy and connection with others. When we recognize the universal human experiences stored in the soul, we can feel closer to others, regardless of surface-level differences. This enables us to establish more authentic and meaningful connections with the people we encounter in our lives.

Empathy is the ability to put ourselves in the shoes of others and understand their emotions and perspectives. When we apply this capacity to our relationships, we become more open to understanding others' experiences. This not only improves the quality of our interactions but can also promote greater harmony in relationships.

*The Soul as an Ethical Guide*

The deepening of the soul can also serve as an ethical guide in our interactions with the world. The soul can provide an internal compass that helps us navigate the moral complexities of life. When we are in tune with the depths of the soul, we develop a sharper sense of what is right and compassion for those who might be affected by our actions.

An individual with a deep connection to the soul is often motivated to make a positive contribution to the world. This can manifest through acts of kindness, community service, social activism, or even through artistic creation that inspires and uplifts others. The soul becomes a source of inspiration and a guiding light in choosing actions that benefit others and the world.

*The Art of Listening to the Souls of Others*

It's not only important to listen to our own soul, but also to learn to listen to the souls of others. Each person has a unique story and a complex inner world. When we pay attention and are truly present with others, we can grasp nuances and depths in their words and actions that we might otherwise overlook. Empathetic listening to the souls of others can create deeper and more meaningful connections in relationships. It means setting aside judgments and assumptions and instead immersing ourselves in the other person's world with respect and curiosity. This kind of listening can lead to greater insight in relationships and the ability to respond more authentically and meaningfully to the needs of others.

*The Soul's Contribution to the World*

Every individual has the potential to make a unique contribution to the world. When we live in harmony with the soul and understand our personal mission, we can contribute significantly to our families, communities, and the entire planet. The soul's contribution to the world can take various forms. Some people may feel called to work for peace, equality, or the environment. Others may express their contribution through art, writing, or the creation of businesses that have a positive impact on society. Regardless of the form it takes, the soul's contribution is guided by a deep understanding of what is meaningful and valuable to the individual.

# INTEGRATING THE DIFFERENT ASPECTS OF THE SOUL: LIGHT AND SHADOW

In our journey through the exploration of the soul, we have delved into the depths of the human psyche, discovering its layers and wonders. However, to fully understand the soul, we must also confront the most complex and multifaceted aspect of human beings: the duality between light and shadow.

## The Soul as a Spectrum of Light and Shadow

The human soul is a mosaic of light and shadow, a symphony of bright virtues and dark imperfections. We often tend to celebrate the light of the soul, its positive and virtuous traits, while concealing or denying its shadow, its darker and more problematic aspects. Yet, it is the integration of both that allows us to fully comprehend who we are.

The light of the soul represents the qualities we admire in ourselves and others. It can include kindness, compassion, generosity, and wisdom. These are the virtues that make us feel closer to our ideal vision of who we should be.

On the other hand, the shadow of the soul consists of those aspects of ourselves that we tend to hide or reject. These can encompass selfishness, anger, jealousy, or fear. Often, these traits are perceived as undesirable or unacceptable.

## The Importance of Integration

But the shadow of the soul should not be feared or rejected. On the contrary, it should be welcomed and integrated.

Integrating the shadow is an act of courage and self-acceptance. It means recognizing that no human being is perfect, and that every individual carries a range of emotions, impulses, and tendencies.

When we integrate the shadow, we become more whole and authentic. It allows us to connect more deeply with ourselves and with others. What was once seen as "negative" becomes a source of understanding and growth. For example, integrated anger can become a driving force for positive change, while integrated fear can lead to greater awareness and caution.

*The Art of Forgiveness and Compassion*

A crucial step in shadow integration is the art of forgiveness, both for others and for ourselves. Often, we carry baggage of resentment, guilt, or shame related to past experiences. These feelings can conceal aspects of the soul's shadow.

Forgiveness does not mean justifying or forgetting what has been done. It means freeing oneself from the emotional weight associated with these experiences. Forgiveness allows us to embrace our past mistakes and those of others as part of the human experience.

Compassion is a companion to forgiveness. When we develop compassion, we acknowledge that every human being is struggling with their own shadow. This recognition enables us to treat others with kindness and understanding, even when they act in ways that may seem incomprehensible.

## The Shadow as a Guide to Growth

The shadow is not just something to run away from but can also serve as a guide to personal growth. When we confront and integrate our shadow, we can learn a lot about ourselves and become more self-aware and compassionate individuals.

One way to explore the shadow is through psychological work and self-inquiry. This can involve reflecting on how we react to stressful situations, exploring our hidden fears and desires, or even keeping a journal to track behavioral patterns that may be connected to the shadow.

## Continuous Integration

The integration of the shadow is an ongoing process because the human psyche is complex and ever-evolving. It requires self-inquiry, reflection, and continuous self-awareness. However, this process can lead to greater authenticity, understanding, and self-love for both ourselves and others.

In the following pages, we will explore the importance of gratitude and celebration in enriching our soul's experience and deepening our connection with the inner world. We will discover how gratitude can serve as a bridge between the light and shadow of the soul, bringing greater joy and satisfaction to our daily lives.

## Continuous Integration

Soul exploration and shadow integration are ongoing processes that require time and dedication. They are akin to an inner journey in which we delve into the depths of our psyche to discover who we truly are. However, the journey does not have a definitive end; it is a continuous path of growth and self-discovery.

## The Art of Gratitude and Celebration

An important aspect of soul exploration is the art of gratitude and celebration. Often, we are so focused on our flaws or the challenges we face that we forget to appreciate the beauty and blessings of life.

Gratitude is like a ray of light that illuminates the soul. It invites us to recognize and appreciate the small daily joys, as well as the greater gifts that life offers us. When practiced regularly, gratitude can change our perspective on life, bringing greater happiness and contentment.

Celebration is a further step in the practice of gratitude. It encourages us to celebrate our victories, both big and small. When we celebrate, we acknowledge our successes and allow ourselves to rejoice in our achievements. This act of celebration can nourish the soul, filling it with joy and pride.

## The Bridge Between Light and Shadow

Gratitude and celebration can serve as a bridge between light and shadow. Often, when we integrate the shadow, we may feel overwhelmed by its more challenging aspects. In those moments, gratitude can be like a guiding light through the darkness.

For example, when we face a period of crisis or personal struggle, the practice of gratitude allows us to find strength and resilience in the challenges we encounter. We can be grateful for the opportunity for growth and learning that the challenge itself offers.

Celebration, on the other hand, can help us recognize our successes and achievements even when they seem overshadowed by the shadow. When we celebrate moments of light and accomplishment, we remind ourselves that the shadow does not define us completely.

*The Hidden Beauty of the Soul*

Finally, as we explore the soul in depth, we may discover a hidden beauty that resides in both the light and the shadow. This beauty is a reflection of our humanity, with all its contradictions and complexities.

Throughout a fascinating and profound journey into the soul, hidden beauty is revealed, an ancient secret that finds a home in both the bright essence and the dark depths. This extraordinary beauty manifests as a delicate reflection of our humanity, a perfect symphony of inherent contradictions and complexities that make up our being.

The human soul unfolds like an intricate and mysterious painting, a canvas that displays vivid colors and shades of deep shadows. Only by contemplating the entire work of art can we truly grasp its inherent magnificence. This requires deep acceptance, an embrace of every facet of our being, without judgment or fear. In this wholeness, our being reveals itself in all its sublime grandeur, unveiling the hidden beauty of the soul in an intriguing dance between light and darkness.

# CHAOTER 6: PRACTICES OF AWARENESS

In the journey toward self-discovery and inner growth, awareness practices play a pivotal role. This chapter is a voyage through the various ways in which we can train our minds and spirits to become more aware, centered, and in harmony with our inner and outer worlds.

## Mindfulness: Being Present in the Here and Now

One of the most well-known and powerful awareness practices is mindfulness, often translated as "awareness" or "mental presence." Mindfulness involves being fully immersed in the present moment, without judgment or projection into the future or past. It's like a focused light on the here and now, illuminating every detail of our current experience.

To cultivate mindfulness, we can begin with the practice of mindfulness meditation. Sitting in silence, we focus on our breath and become aware of each inhalation and exhalation. When thoughts crowd our minds, we observe them as passing clouds in the sky, without clinging to them. This practice helps us develop the ability to observe our thoughts without becoming enslaved by them.

Mindfulness can be extended to all daily activities. We can be mindful while eating, savoring every bite, or while walking, feeling each step and the sensation of the ground beneath our feet.

This practice deeply connects us with our bodies and allows us to fully appreciate the beauty of the present.

## The Art of Meditation

Meditation is another cornerstone of awareness practices. It's a dedicated moment for observing the mind, exploring its depths, and quieting the incessant flow of thoughts. Meditation isn't an attempt to empty the mind but rather to observe it from a detached perspective.

A common practice is insight meditation, which means "seeing things as they are." In this form of meditation, we observe thoughts, emotions, and physical sensations without judgment. We let everything unfold without trying to change or control it. This process helps us develop a profound awareness of ourselves and our automatic reactions.

Meditation can also include guided visualization, where we create mental images that transport us to places of serenity and inspiration. These visualizations can help us relax, relieve stress, and connect with our inner world.

## The Practice of Gratitude

Another mindfulness practice that can transform our lives is gratitude. We often take the small joys and daily blessings for granted. The practice of gratitude invites us to acknowledge and appreciate these things. Each day, we can take a moment to reflect on what we are grateful for.

It could be our health, love, the surrounding nature, or even a simple cup of morning coffee. Gratitude opens us to recognizing life's riches and helps us maintain a positive attitude.

## Exploring Emotions

Emotions are an integral part of our human experience. We often tend to avoid or suppress uncomfortable emotions like anger or sadness, but these emotions are valuable messengers. The mindfulness practice here is to explore emotions without judgment.

When we feel angry, instead of suppressing the emotion, we can ask where this anger is coming from. What is it trying to tell us? Perhaps it's indicating that a personal boundary has been violated or that we need to pay attention to a situation.

Positive emotions can also be explored with mindfulness. When we feel happy, we can inquire about what contributed to this joy and how we can further cultivate it in our lives.

## The Power of Breath

Breath is a constant source of awareness. It is always present, yet we often don't pay it much attention. Taking time to focus on our breath can be a profound mindfulness practice. Breath can be used to calm the mind and relax the body. Through deep breathing, we can send signals to our nervous system to slow down and reduce stress.

Breathing techniques may vary, but a common practice is "conscious breathing." We sit in silence and bring our attention to our breath. We inhale slowly, counting to four, and then exhale in the same measure. This simple act of focusing on the breath can have a significant impact on our awareness.

## Conclusions

Awareness practices serve as an essential bridge between our inner and outer worlds. By embarking on a journey of inner exploration through tools such as mindfulness, meditation, the practice of gratitude, emotional analysis, and attention to breathing, we can cultivate deep self-awareness of ourselves, our emotions, and our thoughts. This journey towards greater self-knowledge not only enriches our inner life but can also lead to significant personal growth that positively influences our relationship with the external world.

# TOOLS AND TECHNIQUES FOR CULTIVATING AWERENESS AND SELF-OBSERVATION

In this chapter, we will dive into the rich world of tools and techniques that can be employed to develop self-awareness and self-observation. These tools act as keys to unlock the doors to our inner world, revealing hidden treasures of wisdom and personal growth.

## *Writing as a Mirror of the Soul*

One of the most powerful techniques for self-observation is writing. Keeping a journal or writing regularly can unveil profound insights into ourselves and our experiences. Writing provides a safe space to explore our thoughts, emotions, and even our dreams.

The practice of reflective writing can take various forms. Some people maintain a daily journal in which they record their daily experiences and reflect upon them. Others prefer to write letters to themselves, exploring deep questions or unresolved issues. Some might even use creative writing to artistically express what would otherwise be challenging to communicate.

Writing is an act of self-observation that allows us to take an impartial look at our minds and hearts. When we put words on paper, we distance ourselves from our thoughts and emotions, enabling us to examine them with clarity.

## *Meditation and Body Awareness*

We have already discussed the importance of meditation, but it's worth delving further into this tool. Meditation is not only a practice for calming the mind but also for developing a profound awareness of our bodies.

An effective meditation technique is body awareness meditation. Sitting in silence, we bring our attention to different parts of our body, starting from the head and moving down to the feet. With gentleness and non-judgment, we observe the physical sensations that arise in each area of the body.

This practice helps bridge the gap between the mind and the body, revealing how emotions manifest physically. For example, we might discover that tension in the jaw is linked to our anxiety, or that a light feeling in the stomach is associated with moments of joy.

## The "Third Eye" Technique

Another powerful tool for self-observation is known as the "third eye" technique. This has nothing to do with the physical eye but refers to the opening of an inner eye, a deeper and more intuitive perception of reality.

The "third eye" technique involves focusing on the area between the eyebrows, often associated with the "third eye" in Eastern systems of thought. By closing our eyes and directing our attention to this area, we can develop a greater awareness of our intuitions and inner perceptions.

This technique can be used to explore profound questions or gain a clearer insight into the situations we are experiencing. It works best when we are relaxed and open to intuition.

## The Practice of Compassion

Compassion is a powerful tool for self-observation and personal growth. We often tend to be very hard on ourselves, harshly judging our mistakes and imperfections. The practice of compassion involves offering ourselves the same kindness and understanding that we would extend to a friend.

When we feel judged or guilty, we can pause and ask ourselves, "What would we say to a friend in this situation?" The response is often very different from how we treat ourselves. Compassion invites us to treat ourselves with kindness, forgive ourselves for our mistakes, and cultivate self-love.

## The Path of Art and Creativity

Art and creativity are powerful ways to express our inner world. Creative endeavors can reveal hidden aspects of ourselves and provide a path to explore complex emotions.

You don't need to be a skilled artist to benefit from this technique. You can draw, paint, write poetry, dance, or even cook with mindfulness. What matters is the creative process and the authentic expression of what lies within us.

## Conclusions

The tools and techniques for developing awareness and self-observation are diverse and offer multiple opportunities. Each of us can choose the practices that resonate most with our nature and growth journey. For instance, writing serves as a mirror for our thoughts and emotions, allowing us to explore our inner world through words. Meditation, on the other hand, provides a path to delve into the depths of the mind and discover inner tranquility. Body awareness connects us to physical sensations, linking us to our bodily essence and helping us recognize important signals.

The "third eye" technique encourages us to explore the subtler dimension of consciousness, opening the door to deep insights. Additionally, compassion allows us to nurture loving relationships with ourselves and others, while creative expression unleashes our imagination and lets us give voice to our deepest feelings. In short, these paths represent gateways leading to our inner world, offering valuable tools for deepening self-understanding and personal growth. Consciously choosing these practices can be a significant step in constructing our inner journey.

# MEDITATION, MINDFULNESS, AND OTHER PRACTICES FOR CONNECTING WITH THE MIND'S ECHO

In the hectic and distracted world we live in, finding time for reflection and connecting with our inner world can seem like a challenge. However, in this chapter, we will explore various practices, including meditation, mindfulness, and other forms of introspection, that allow us to immerse ourselves in the echo of the mind meaningfully and sustainably.

## Meditation: The Art of Observation

Meditation is one of the oldest and most powerful practices for accessing our inner world. It is an art that involves observing the mind without judgment. Often, in the fast-paced rhythms of daily life, we are caught up in our thoughts, overwhelmed by our emotions, and confused by our concerns. Meditation offers us a pause, a space of calm where we can become observers of our thoughts.

To begin a meditation practice, find a quiet place, sit comfortably, and close your eyes. Focus on your breath. Observe the breath as it enters and leaves your body. When your mind begins to wander, as it inevitably will, gently redirect your attention to your breath. Do not judge your thoughts or emotions; simply accept them as they are.

Meditation is not an art mastered instantly. It takes time and patience. But with consistent practice, you can develop a greater awareness of your thoughts, emotions, and the echo of the mind that contains them.

## Mindfulness: Living in the Present Moment

Mindfulness is a practice closely related to meditation but can be integrated into daily life in practical ways. It means being aware and present in the current moment, rather than getting lost in the past or worrying about the future.

A common mindfulness practice is to fully focus on what you are doing, whether you are eating, walking, or even washing the dishes. Too often, we are physically present but mentally absent, unable to fully experience the beauty and richness of life.

Mindfulness invites us to slow down, to perceive every sensation, every scent, every sound. It is a way to break free from the frenzy and establish a deep connection with our inner world and what surrounds us.

## Introspective Practices

In addition to meditation and mindfulness, there are many other introspective practices that can help us connect with the echo of the mind. One of these is the practice of powerful questions. Set aside time to reflect on meaningful questions such as, "Who am I truly?" "What is my purpose in life?" "What genuinely makes me happy?"

Keep a journal of your reflections and discoveries. Writing the answers to these questions can reveal deep aspects of yourself that you may have never explored.

Other introspective practices include art, dance, music, and reading. Every form of creative expression can serve as a bridge between the conscious and unconscious mind, allowing the echo of the mind to emerge through art.

*Sharing and Empathetic Listening*

Let's not forget the importance of sharing and empathetic listening in introspective practices. By discussing our thoughts and emotions with others, we can gain a different perspective and discover new dimensions of the echo of the mind. Empathetic listening, in turn, allows us to better understand others and broaden our worldview.

In conclusion, there are various paths to explore the echo of the mind. Meditation and mindfulness serve as powerful tools for observing thoughts, while introspective practices and creative expression allow us to give voice to what we find within. Whether you prefer the serenity of meditation or the creative energy of art, these methodologies will guide you in delving into the depths of your inner world.

# CHAPTER 7: TRANSFORMATION AND REALIZATION

In the journey of exploring the echo of the mind, we have delved into the depths of the soul and consciousness, confronted both the shadow and the light, and acquired mindfulness practices to connect with our inner world. In this chapter, we will immerse ourselves in the very essence of personal transformation and realization.

## The Birth of Transformation

Personal transformation doesn't commence with lightning or an epiphanic event but with awareness. It's the moment when we recognize the need for change, growth, or evolution. This awareness can arise from a sense of dissatisfaction, the challenge of a crisis, or simply the quest for a more meaningful life.

One of the keys to transformation is acceptance – acknowledging that we are imperfect and that change is a gradual journey. We often attempt to change ourselves through sheer willpower, but true transformation necessitates kindness towards oneself and the ability to learn from our mistakes.

## The Mind as Alchemist

Throughout history, many cultures have adopted the image of the alchemist as a metaphor for the process of inner transformation. In ancient alchemy, the plumbum philosophorum, the raw material, was transmuted into gold through a long and complex process. In our quest for self-realization, the mind itself can be seen as the alchemist. Through awareness and understanding of our thoughts, emotions, and behaviors, we can transform aspects of ourselves that may seem like "raw material" into gold, into wisdom, compassion, and inner growth.

*The Power of Choice*

Personal realization is closely tied to the power of choice. Every day, we are presented with countless decisions, some of which can shape the course of our lives. However, we often move through life automatically, lacking awareness of the choices we make.

Making conscious decisions requires deep introspection. It means exploring our beliefs, values, and desires. This requires courage, as we may discover that some of our past choices were not authentic or meaningful.

*Realization and Connection*

Personal realization is not a solitary journey. Although the echo of the mind resonates deeply within each of us, we find meaning and fulfillment in interaction with others and the world around us.

Relationships play a crucial role in our transformational journey. Through interaction and connection with others, we can discover new perspectives and receive support in the challenges we face.

Personal realization is also an act of generosity. When we achieve realization, we can share it with others, inspiring them and contributing to the common good.

*The Endless Journey*

It is essential to emphasize that the path to transformation and self-realization has no defined final destination. There is no point where we can claim to have reached a definitive completion. Realization represents an endless journey, a constant expansion of our awareness and authenticity, in which we are in perpetual evolution.

In this chapter, we have only scratched the surface of this intricate theme of personal transformation and self-realization. Each of us must embark on our own journey, navigating through the challenges and precious opportunities that life presents.

In the following pages, we will explore in-depth how we can put these concepts into practice to shape a life of meaning and contribute to the well-being of the world around us. It will be a journey of continuous discovery and growth, where we embrace awareness as a companion and commit to shaping our destiny with wisdom and intention.

## THE POTENTIAL FOR PERSONAL GROWTH AND DEVELOPMENT THROUGH INTROSPECTION

In our journey through the realm of the mind's echo, we have explored the depths of the soul, unveiled age-old secrets, and acquired practices of mindfulness. However, a central concept we've merely touched upon is the limitless potential for personal growth and development that lies within us, ready to be unlocked through introspection.

*Introspection as the Key to Transformation*

Introspection is the process through which we critically and reflectively examine our thoughts, emotions, behaviors, and experiences. It's like possessing a magic lantern that illuminates the dark depths of our minds. But what is the true power of introspection?

1. *Deep Self-Awareness:*

Through introspection, we become aware of our automatic thought patterns, innate emotional reactions, and habitual behaviors. This deep awareness is the first step toward any form of change or personal growth.

2. *Self-Acceptance:*

Often, in the process of introspection, we discover parts of ourselves that may not align with the ideal image we have of ourselves. However, introspection teaches us to accept these parts without judgment. We realize that perfection isn't the goal; growth is.

3. *Creative Outlet:*

Introspection can unlock the dormant creative potential within each of us. When we explore the recesses of our minds, we may discover new ideas, inspirations, and creative solutions to the challenges we encounter.

4. *Emotion Management:*

Introspection teaches us to better manage our emotions. When we understand the roots of our emotions, we are better equipped to regulate our emotional responses in stressful or challenging situations.

5. *Relationship Development:*

Introspection doesn't stop with ourselves; it can also enhance our relationships with others. When we better understand ourselves, we become more empathetic and understanding towards others. This capacity for deeper connection can significantly improve relational dynamics.

*Introspection in Action*

So, how can we use introspection to unlock our potential for personal growth and development? Here are some practices that can help us on this journey:

1. *Personal Journal:*

Keeping a journal where we jot down our thoughts, emotions, and daily experiences can be an effective way to deepen introspection.

2. *Meditation and Mindfulness:*

Meditation and mindfulness help us develop greater self-awareness and awareness of our present experiences.

3. *Inner Dialogue:*

Asking deep questions and listening to answers from within can help us explore our core beliefs and deepest desires.

4. *Dream Analysis:*

Dreams can be windows into the depths of our minds. Keeping a dream journal and analyzing them can reveal hidden meanings.

5. *Therapy or Coaching:*

Working with a psychotherapist or an experienced coach can provide valuable guidance in introspective exploration and realizing one's potential.

*Reaching the Infinite Within Us*

Deep within each individual lies infinite potential for personal growth and development. Introspection is the key to unlocking this wealth. However, the journey is highly personal, and everyone will find their unique way to harness this powerful tool. Introspection allows us to explore personal thoughts, emotions, and experiences, confronting fears and revealing new perspectives.

There's no one-size-fits-all path for introspection; some may prefer meditation, others writing, or other forms of creative expression. In any case, this endless journey guides us to discover and embrace the richness of our inner world, promoting personal growth and authenticity.

## INTEGRATING INNER EXPERIENCE INTO EVERYDAY LIFE

We have navigated the deep waters of introspection, explored the labyrinth of our minds, and discovered hidden treasures within our souls. But what does it really mean to bring this inner experience into everyday life? How can we translate the awareness we've gained into tangible action? In this chapter, we will examine how we can integrate our inner growth into our daily existence.

*Integration as a Bridge Between Inward and Outward*

Inner experience is intrinsically linked to our external life. However, unless we learn how to connect these two worlds, our inner growth runs the risk of lingering in the limbo of abstraction. Here's how we can build a strong bridge between our inner world and our daily life:

1. *Continuous Awareness:*

The first step is to maintain continuous self-awareness, keeping track of our emotions and reactions as we navigate daily challenges. This requires constant practice, but over time, it becomes a habit that leads to greater awareness.

2. *Awareness Rituals:*

Incorporating small awareness rituals into your day can make a difference. For example, you can start your morning with a few minutes of meditation or mindfulness to set the stage for a mindful day.

3. *Gratitude Practice:*

Gratitude is a powerful way to connect your inner world with your external life. Each day, reflect on what you're thankful for and express that gratitude. This will help you maintain a positive perspective.

4. *Informed Action:*

Inner growth should inform your actions. For instance, if introspection reveals a need to improve your communication skills, commit to actions that develop this competence.

5. *Conscious Choice:*

Awareness gives you the power to make conscious choices. Before reacting impulsively, take a moment to reflect and choose how you want to respond to a situation.

*A Life Guided by Awareness*

When you integrate inner experience into your daily life, your existence becomes more meaningful and centered. Here are some ways this integration can enhance your life:

- **Greater Emotional Balance***: Awareness of your emotions helps you manage them better, leading to greater emotional stability.
- **Healthier Relationships***: Self-understanding allows you to better understand others, improving your interpersonal relationships.
- **Professional Success:** *Awareness of your strengths and areas of growth can enhance your performance at work.*

- ***Physical and Mental Well-being:*** Stress management and promoting a healthy lifestyle are natural extensions of inner growth.
- ***Personal Fulfillment:*** When you are aligned with your true self, you tend to make choices and take actions that lead you toward deeper and more authentic fulfillment.

*A Constant Cycle of Growth*

Integrating inner experience into everyday life is not a destination but rather a continuous cycle of growth. As you put these habits and approaches into practice, you'll be able to face daily challenges with greater serenity and wisdom.

## CONCLUSION: AN ENDLESS JOURNEY INTO THE EXPLORATION OF MIND AND SPIRIT

Our journey through the depths of the soul in search of the echo of the mind now reaches a turning point. We have explored personal introspection, inner growth, and practices of mindfulness, delving into the recesses of our psyche and opening the doors to transformation. But the journey doesn't end here; instead, we are at the beginning of an infinite and captivating adventure.

The experience of exploring the mind and spirit is like opening an endless book, with pages of knowledge and wisdom unfolding infinitely. Each day can bring a new revelation, a fresh insight, a deeper understanding of oneself.

Introspection and inner growth demand time and dedication. Just as an explorer doesn't give up at the first difficulty, so must the seeker of inner truth persevere despite challenges.

During our journey, we have touched upon the concept of the connection between soul, spirit, and consciousness. As we continue along the path, we will discover that this connection extends beyond ourselves to embrace the world and the universe. Every step in our growth journey contributes to collective awareness.

As we gain awareness of ourselves, we also become more attuned to others. Compassion becomes a natural gift, as we understand that we are all on our individual journeys. This compels us to be kind, empathetic, and supportive.

In the preceding chapters, we have seen how personal introspection can lead to profound transformation. Continuing the journey, we recognize our responsibility in shaping not only our own lives but also the world around us.

The path of personal introspection is an endless journey. It is an eternal dance between self-exploration and the quest for deeper spiritual understanding, between observing the mind and seeking a greater comprehension of the spirit. Each step forward brings us closer to a more complete realization of ourselves and connects us to something greater than the individual.

As you continue your journey, remember that your personal development is not a selfish act. It is a contribution to the well-being of the world. When one person is illuminated with understanding and wisdom, they radiate light to others as well. Your inner growth can positively influence those around you and, ultimately, impact society as a whole.

I conclude this volume with an enigmatic final invitation. Whether you are at the beginning of this mysterious path or have already traversed numerous stages, remember that you are never alone in this adventure. As explorers of knowledge and truth, we travel together, contributing to transforming the world into a place suffused with awareness, compassion, and inspiration.

I encourage you to continue to plumb the depths of your understanding, both of yourself and the surrounding world. Through mastery of the mind and the power of the spirit, you have the potential to leave an indelible mark on the history of humanity.

Your journey is a precious and unique gem. May it be enriched with astonishing discoveries, loving kindness, and personal realization.

In the understanding that we are all connected, I bid you farewell with a sense of profound connection as you continue on your extraordinary journey, through the echo of the mind.

The End

# AUTHOR INFORMATION

*Francesco Baldi, originally from Florence, is an eclectic professional with a deep passion for technology, art, and writing. In addition to his current position as an IT specialist, web designer, SEO expert, and digital marketer, Francesco demonstrates extraordinary creativity as a content creator and possesses an in-depth knowledge of the latest technologies. He develops innovative and original projects that have established him as a reference in his field.*

*But his versatility extends beyond the realm of IT: Francesco also nurtures a great passion for scientific writing, storytelling, and novels, showcasing remarkable storytelling skills. The deep dedication and passion he invests in both disciplines are reflected in the extraordinary results he achieves in his work and his literary, artistic, and design creations.*

*His ability to combine these two passions has allowed him to explore new horizons of knowledge and create original and engaging works that bring out the best in his creative and technical abilities. With his intellectual curiosity and constant determination to improve, Francesco continues to inspire and be inspired continuously.*